AMERICA'S GAME GIRL

This book is dedicated to both of my Grandmother's Louise Garner & Karen Brown. To my Grandfather's Neil "Red" Hill and Louis Maddison Jones (never met) and Calvin Brown (Grandpa). To my family members and friends, Rosetta Garner, Monique Scott, Quinton "Popeye" Verdun, Vince Bledsoe, Clarice Brown, Sidney Garner, auntie Cynthia, Felicia Wilson, Anthony McMichael, Andrew "Bubby" Muse, Erica Lang, Zsanita "Michelle" Woodard, Jessica Woodson, Brandie Marie Joyner, Tammy Barnes, Andrea Gray (friend & #1 Braider) Erica Baxter (who called me her bi-polar baby), Joesph 'Tomar' Peoples, Gwendolyn Perkins, Charles Edward Smith III, Tijon Champ, Cameron "baby" TC" Hurndon, Amanda Rabb, Anthony Harold, Willie "Trip" Ford, Melissa Chambers, Talisa Smith, Rodney Stevens ("lil Rodney"), Mentor T. Rodgers (Sometimes Me, sometimes you, Always Us 1,2,1,2), Mentor "General Jeff" Page. To everyone who has battled or is currently battling with Mental Health and Substance use disorder. To the ones who have succumbed to their addiction or died by Suicide. Most importantly, to the man who instilled and enforced the value of education, integrity and structure.

To The Father who "Stepped Up",

Mr. Quintin McMichael Sr.

THANK YOU, "POP"

America's Game Girl

BRIDGING THE GAPS
A JOURNEY OF LOVE,
MENTAL HEALTH, AND
OVERCOMING STIGMA

Teri Rushawn Rogers

Breaking Stigmas Treatment Operation 501(c)3 Nonprofit Organization

Contents

INTRODUCTION

As the echoes of the past reverberate within me, I am reminded of the meaningful impact the film "Game Girls" had on me, as it unveiled the raw essence of existence in the desolate Skid Row. The maelstrom of turmoil and adversity depicted on screen strikes a familiar chord in my heart because it is a portion of my journey. From wrestling with the shadows of my mind to battle with the harsh grip of substance abuse and the cruel embrace of homelessness, I have gleaned firsthand insight into the intricate tapestry of these societal dilemmas and the stifling stigma that shrouds them.

Nevertheless, amidst the tempestuous trials I have weathered, I stand defiantly proud to proclaim that I have journeyed a considerable distance. Two years ago, I summoned the courage to embark upon an audacious endeavor, birthing a non-profit organization with the noble intention of dismantling the detrimental stereotypes clutching tightly to mental health, substance abuse, and homelessness. This path I tread has been strewn with alarming challenges, yet it has yielded immeasurable rewards.

Through my humanitarian organization, I have extended a compassionate hand to countless souls ensnared in comparable plights to my former tribulations. My narrative has taught me the privileged significance of emotional well-being, the significant mantle of accountability, the transformative force of acceptance, the enduring power of love, the fragile essence of trust, the unforgettable scars of triggers, the pervasive specter of trauma, the invaluable art of respect, the sincere truthfulness of communication, and the enriching depths of comprehension. These deep themes, which have gracefully interwoven with the fabric of my existence and my journey, are the very topics I yearn to explore within this literary offering, as they have shaped my life's trajectory in thorough measure.

Reflecting, I am reminded of the shattered connections and their intense impact on my cognitive well-being. The undulating waves of affection, the intricacies of navigating intimate bonds while fighting with personal adversities, and the significance of open and empathetic communication all come to the foreground. In the film "Game Girls," I encountered the turbulent nature of relationships amidst trying circumstances.

The undersupply of monetary resources, or rather the absence thereof, persistently inflicted distress during my most somber hours. Financial instability not only intensified my psychological afflictions but also added another layer of difficulties to my trials. Amidst the fierce realms of poverty and substance dependency, seeking stability and security was an exhausted need nevertheless, I obtained the vital wisdom of carefully managing funds, continuing my education and seeking financial aid when necessary, and cultivating a healthy accord with monetary matters to forge a better future.

Substance abuse, a cure upon which I relied in my cloudiest moments in time, granted a brief pause from the anguish and strife trap me. Yet, in due course, it intensified my predicament, plunging me deeper into the abyss. Overcoming addiction proved to be a challenging expedition, one that stood as an indispensable milestone on my path to recovery and personal growth. It necessitated an honest confrontation with my triggers, a poignant acknowledgment of my trauma, and a passionate pursuit of professional assistance. Moreover, it imparted valuable lessons on the significance of self-nurturance and the pursuit of wholesome coping mechanisms to navigate the turbulence of emotions and pressures. The maze of the legal realm presented yet another daunting obstacle on my rigorous path. The involvement and complexity of the legal system seemed specifically designed to confound and intimidate those already marginalized and vulnerable. Determined to overcome these challenges, I immersed myself in the complexity of my rights, sought legal aid whenever necessary, and steadfastly advocated for myself. The path was treacherous, but it bestowed upon me a great appreciation for comprehending the law and harnessing its resources to safeguard my rights and safeguard my interests.

Amidst my exciting journey, my sexuality was yet another facet of my existence impacted by manifold struggles. As I wrestled with the harrowing complexities of mental health, substance abuse, and home-lessness, I simultaneously navigated the puzzle of my desires. The path proved filled with hardship, as I confronted discrimination and preju-dice piled upon me by a society averse to such diversity. Nevertheless, this grim quest taught me the paramount significance of embracing self-acceptance and self-love, while creating a supportive community that champions inclusivity and embraces the collection of human ex-perience.

As my journey unfolded, I gradually comprehended the keen grav-ity of addressing the deep-rooted traumas that too often underpin the cycles of mental anguish, substance dependency, and homelessness. These traumas, relentless in their manifestation, cast an unrelenting shadow upon one's emotional well-being. The painful journey towards recovery and growth necessitates raw courage and daring vulnerabil-ity, as one confronts and heals from these indelible scars. Through the transformative power of therapy, counseling, and a nurturing network of support, I have discovered the strength to confront and acknowl-edge these traumas, embarking on an expedition towards healing and resilience.

Homelessness

In the intricate shade of existence, homelessness emerges as a complicated problem, a riddle woven from various threads: poverty, unemployment, mental anguish, and addiction. Within this tangled web, those entangled in the throes of homelessness often find themselves embattled with insurmountable obstacles in pursuit of respite and redemption. "Game Girls," the cinematic creation, artfully reveals a portion of my life as I navigate the treacherous terrain of a relationship whilst dwelling amidst the destitution of Skid Row, the notorious enclave nestled in downtown Los Angeles that teems with the disenfranchised souls cut off from shelter.

To embark upon this journey of homelessness is to confront one's fragility, a stark vulnerability laid bare in the face of meager resources. Yet, I, fortunate enough to be cradled by a cocoon of support during such wild times, have resolved to extend a helping hand through my philanthropic venture. Like a beacon in the tempest, my non-profit organization endeavors to furnish the destitute with resources and bolster their fortitude, guiding them toward liberation from the clutches of their distressing predicament.

Chief among the manifold tribulations that afflict the unhoused is the absence of a steadfast place to call home. Deprived of a haven, they struggle with an onslaught of adversities, be it nature's merciless elements, hindrances in accessing vital aid, or stopping one of their sense of security. Through my zealous enterprise, we stand ready to offer transient housing alternatives to those trapped in this pervasive crisis, striving ceaselessly to forge pathways towards more sustainable, enduring dwellings that shelter them from the continual storm.

In addition to providing referrals to shelter, we strive to offer a multitude of avenues for individuals enduring the plight of homelessness to regain stability. We extend our reach to include valuable provisions such as occupational training initiatives, educational facilities, and comprehensive mental health as well as addiction services. Indeed, substance abuse and psychological adversities oftentimes afflict those cast into homelessness, hence addressing these emergencies becomes all the more imperative to facilitate their triumph over such adverse circumstances.

Not only do we extend our aid to solitary individuals, but we also acknowledge the particular challenges faced by families who find themselves in the treacherous realm of homelessness. We endeavor to cater to their unique needs, offering resources ranging from childcare provisions to educational support for the vulnerable children intertwined with the crisis.

Overall, homelessness invades our society, presenting a complex challenge to overcome. It is through my non-profit organization that I diligently work towards providing an extensive array of resources and unfaltering support for both individuals and families submerged in homelessness. Additionally, I strive to tear down the collective biases and prejudgments that shackle this issue. Homelessness can befall anyone, irrespective of their background or circumstances. It is necessary to grasp the essence of their humanity, recognizing their core worth, and assuring that those in need receive the vital assistance and resources required to break free from the clutches of such adversity.

"Skidrow is a world in a world"
Teri Rogers 2014

Mental Health

In recent times, the notion of mental well-being has assumed a pivotal position in societal discourse, as an increasing number of individuals are sharing their tough battles with diverse mental afflictions. Regrettably, despite this burgeoning attention, mental health remains burdened with stigma, instilling in numerous individuals fear of seeking comfort or expressing their tribulations. I, too, am ensnared within this difficulty; a long period laced with disgrace at my mental affliction, and a fear that others shall abuse me harshly.

As I thread through the complex maze of existence, I navigate many psychological weaknesses encompassing desolation, apprehension, and psychological trauma. These continual worries have cast their dark cloud over my relationships, tough pursuits, and, ultimately, my overarching state of well-being. At times, I find myself submerged in a menacing chaos of emotions, confronted with what seems to be an impossible escape. Yet, an unyielding truth emerged from this abyss of despair - a potent realization that compelled me to contemplate the flaw of perpetuating this mode of existence and impelled me to gracefully advocate for myself as well as others, so I began to seek aid.

I set about upon a therapeutic adventure, guided by an insightful counselor who illuminated the dark corridors of my emotions, furnishing me with indispensable strategies to navigate their volatile region. Additionally, I sought solace in congregations of kindred spirits, individuals dealing with similar psychological turmoil. These sanctuaries of shared vulnerability served as a cohesive structure of companionship, shattering the asphyxiating stream of isolation. Furthermore, I assumed the mantle of self-care, embracing activities that fostered my well-being - exercises invigorating my mortal frame, the serenity of meditation, and immersive communion with the natural world - all attaining the divine effect of alleviating stressors, thus uplifting the totality of my being.

Integrated into this enduring retreat, I grasped the deep significance of mental health advocacy and the strong potency of enunciating our load. Mental afflictions should never become a label of fragility, bereaving individuals of their inherent worth; rather, it is a broad mark of strength to seek the assistance needed for convalescence. Therefore, I cast my acclamation towards mental health cognizance, entreating others to unveil the shackles of silence and resolutely embrace the opportunity to solicit the relief they so deserve.

2016
Teri Rogers

Substance Use Disorder

Substance Use Disorder, an overpowering challenge that plagues individuals across all social spheres, finds itself hidden in a haze of stigma and misconception. Consequently, those scuffle with addiction encounter a severe challenge in their quest for assistance. Within the realm of the film "Game Girls," one character emerges as one who seems at ease within the subterranean realm of Skid Row's economy, wherein drugs assume prominence as both a commodity and a currency. Conversely, I yearn to sever ties with this existence, aspiring to elevate my circumstances.

I too have faced my conflict with substance use disorder, a period of unfathomable darkness that cast its darkening cloud over my mental fortitude, relationships, and overall well-being. Yet, as I launched on a quest for recovery and personal enlightenment, I became informed on the fact that my addiction to substance usage is not a mere testament to moral frailty, but rather a ailment necessitating empathy, understanding, and above all, unwavering support. Though the road was purposeful in its challenges, invaluable lessons I obtained along the way shed light upon the significance of self-compassion and the subtle impact of seeking solace in others. Thus, my firm commitment lies in shattering the prejudiced perceptions surrounding substance abuse, while serving as a bastion of support for those entwined in a similar struggle.

Indeed, my voyage through the web of substance use disorder has birthed an urge within me to establish a non-profit organization that focuses its efforts on breaking the stigmas that invariably cling to addiction. Our organization endeavors, through education, advocacy, and community outreach, to revolutionize the narrative surrounding addiction, bring about a climate of understanding, while simultaneously offering resources to individuals and families ensnared by its voracious grip.

In the realm of our organization's conviction lies a resolute determination to grant access to treatments grounded in tangible evidence, most notably therapy and support groups. Furthermore, we are passionate patrons of resources that facilitate this therapeutic journey. An unyielding adherence to the concept of recovery, and the recognition of its inherent potency, fuels our mission to ensure that no individual faces the burdens of addiction in seclusion. Our collaborative efforts are entwined with healthcare providers, policymakers, and community leaders, as we ardently champion policies that place addiction treatment and recovery services at the tip of prioritization. Prying apart the shackles of association with substance abuse and addiction - breaking the stifling stigmas - occupies a pivotal position within the core tenets of our enterprise. The time has dawned upon us to part ways with prejudiced sentiments and prejudgments, endeavoring instead to perceive addiction as an affliction that seeks solace within the realm of public health - one that necessitates boundless empathy and unwavering support. Through fostering an environment of comprehension and relief we confront the paramount goal of empowering individuals to seek support and guidance, thus embarking on a life permeated with purpose and satisfaction. Additionally, our organization extends its arms, offering a diverse range of services that encompass an array of challenges faced within our community. Mental Health First Aid training, accompanied by certification, serves as an invaluable knowledge acquisition in this pursuit of communal welfare. Besides, First Time Homebuyers Workshops, domestic violence support catering to both survivors and victims' alike, as well as comprehensive life insurance and burial policies, all converge to reiterate our unwavering dedication to fulfilling the immense needs that exist within our community.

News interview on SKIDROW
Teri Rogers 2018

Money

The unsafe state of one's finances and the widespread plague of poverty can wield a skilled influence on an individual's overall well-being, seeping into the depths of their mental and physical health. Creating a firm foundation of financial stability presents an intimidating challenge, indeed. Breaking the relentless cycle of destitution proves a wearisome task, particularly when confronted with scarce opportunities and meager resources. Nevertheless, through my non-profit organization, I toil ceaselessly to furnish those in need with the financial assistance and knowledge they crave. This uphill endeavor entails hosting workshops focused on the art of budgeting, financial planning, debt management and credit building.

Yet, it is not solely financial education that our organization imparts; we also endeavor to equip individuals with the tools necessary for vocational training and gainful employment. We comprehend the intricate link between financial stability and gainful work, thus striving to furnish indigent souls with a viable opportunity to sever the chains of poverty and embrace the prospect of fiscal freedom.

Furthermore, the essence of our mission lies in cultivating a cohesive community where individuals are infused with a newfound sense of empowerment, enabling them to seize command of their economic destiny. Firmly convinced that knowledge and resources are the twin catalysts for informed financial decision-making and successful goal attainment, we employ every resource at our disposal to liberate those ensnared by poverty's grip. Our ultimate aspiration is to dismantle the shackles of destitution, forging a path toward enduring financial stability and independence for all souls trapped in its treacherous web.

The inescapable reality remains that financial instability and destitution are alarming fighters, wielding consequences that reverberate far and wide. Skid Row, a violent realm wherein these terrifying challenges hold reign, becomes a crucible wherein the provision of resources and unwavering support to those in need assumes vital importance. As Founder of Breaking Stigmas Treatment Operation, I steadfastly strive to deliver the financial resources and education, alongside vocational training and employment prospects, that may serve as lifelines to those surrounded by the mark of financial instability and poverty. Armed with a nurturing community and an arsenal of tools and resources that breed success, we shall empower individuals to transcend the shackles of destitution and seize their rightful throne of financial independence.

2014 DTLA
Teri Rogers

Law

Unexpectedly emerging legal matters can bear significant consequences on our existence. Nevertheless, for those in the tribulations of poverty and homelessness, the perplexing web of the law and justice system can prove all the more demoralizing and harsher to bridge. Many unfortunate souls who have experienced destitution and homelessness may be deprived of the means to legal counsel or awareness of their entitlements, leaving them vulnerable to legal setbacks and complete injustices.

Likewise, I have personally confronted legal predicaments in times past, providing me intimate insight into the hardships of maneuvering the justice system in need of substantial resources and support. However, through the establishment of Breaking Stigmas Treatment Operation, I work non-stop to offer the underprivileged access to legal aid and the necessary support. Our organization takes pride in providing legal clinics, workshops, and connections to compassionate attorneys, all critical in aiding individuals in procuring legal assistance and proficiently navigating the tangled network of justice.

In acting with this, we diligently educate individuals on their basic legal rights and equip them with the resources essential to comprehend and navigate the complex legal processes. Our unyielding belief believes that every individual deserves the right to equal access to justice, regardless of their socio-economic standing, rendering it our solemn duty to empower these individuals with the necessary knowledge and resources to avidly advocate for themselves and their communities.

Undoubtedly, confronted with legal obstacles may cause a flood of anxiety and/or depression, yet armed with appropriate resources and unwavering support, one can artfully advocate for oneself and overcome the complexities of justice. Through the legal resources and support afforded by our organization, our sincere hope remains that the barriers, impeding individuals from seizing their right to justice, may be shattered, thereby ensuring that every person possesses an equitable opportunity to exercise their important legal rights.

Sex

Sexuality and intimate connections constitute twisted facets of our existence—territory that can prove challenging and complicated to navigate, particularly when our perspectives and principles diverge from those of our partners. The cinematic masterpiece, "Game Girls," lays bare the relationship, shadowed by their conflicting attitudes toward sex work. Such a narrative mirrors the reality of countless relationships wherein companions harbor differing values and ideologies regarding intimacy and partnership.

For a very long time, I scuffled with allocating gratification to my boundaries and requirements within my sexual liaisons, which culminated in numerous dissatisfying and distasteful encounters. Nonetheless, through therapeutic activities, I organized and prioritized my boundaries and needs within these groups. I gradually grasped that upholding my boundaries and asserting my needs was key to cultivating nourishing relationships —unveiling the bedrock for maintaining healthy and gratifying bonds.

Furthermore, sexual well-being assumes a paramount role in our overall welfare, yet it regrettably remains a subject steeped in stigma and disregard. Multitudes of individuals suffer from humiliation, criticism, and prejudice while endeavoring to access resources and education on sexual health. This calamitous reality results in dire consequences, comprising sexually transmitted infections, unwanted pregnancies, and toxic sexual entanglements.

Thus, prioritizing sexual health education assumes imperativeness, and within my public-spirited organization, we labor vigorously to break the stigmas encasing sexual well-being, simultaneously extending resources to the needy. Our nest offers comprehensive education and unwavering support to individuals across all spectrums, orientations, and backgrounds—an impartial haven where all are embraced, nurtured and free from discrimination.

Failed Relationships and Self Love

For a considerable duration, my relationships were characterized by sensation, disorder, and rides of emotional intensity. Frequently, I would find myself immersed in volatile entanglements, riddled with strife. My lack of confidence and self-worth drove me to embrace partners who were distant emotionally, and at times, even abusive or I was the abuser. I invested an abundance of time, energy, and sentiment into these relations, yearning for my chosen companion to metamorphose into the embodiment of affection I envisioned.

Nevertheless, this recurring pattern of conduct merely birthed heartache and agony. I would often emerge from these alliances more despondent than before, only to repeat the cycle with each new suitor. It was solely upon reaching the depth of my existence that the epiphany struck me, compelling recognition of my obligation to assume responsibility for my actions and welfare, to shatter this continuous pattern.

Embarking upon a path of therapy, reflection, and knowledge gaining, I delved into the significance of accountability, acceptance, and communication within the realm of relationships. I comprehended the necessity of assuming accountability for my deeds and emotions, emancipating myself from the reliance on a partner's validation of my true value. Moreover, I grasped the imperative task of embracing my authentic self, embracing both my perfections and imperfections, rather than striving to conform to another's ideal of flawlessness.

Furthermore, I unearthed the paramount significance of effective communication within a healthy partnership. I endeavored to express my desires and boundaries lucidly and respectfully, while concurrently assimilating my partner's needs and concerns. This endeavor propelled my connections towards a sincere level of understanding and trust, an experience once unfamiliar to me.

Through these hard-fought lessons, the very fiber of my relationships and my emotional landscape has undergone an insightful transformation. I have come to embrace the empowering notion that severing ties with toxic bonds is not only acceptable but necessary for the preservation of my mental equilibrium. A revelation now firmly etched in the deepest recesses of my soul, I have apprehended that authenticity, vulnerability, and unreserved communication and comprehension lay the foundation of genuine trust and love.

In the admired sanctuary I now find myself, a haven of comfort and nurturance within self, I thrive within the embrace of self. Today, I truly love and cherish the essence of my being. Deep gratitude surges within me for the transformative lessons I have passionately acquired and the personal growth I have created. The trials and tribulations have artfully molded the very essence of my being, giving me the fortitude and clarity to inspire others immersed in comparable struggles.

A cardinal epiphany that has come to the fore is the momentous realization of tending to my emotional well-being. An imperative that demands precedence, safeguarding my cerebral sanctity assumes vital importance as I endeavor to navigate an ambiguous world that begs conformity and compromise. My journey of self-discovery has formed an understanding that durable and flourishing relationships are extremely founded upon respect, unfettered communication, and compassionate comprehension. Moreover, I have learned that laying out clear boundaries and prioritizing the mercy of my well-being are divine views of self-actualization.

In the silence of reflection, my heart overflows with gratitude and reverence for the bountiful love and unwavering support that floods me with the responsibility of my present union. A stark departure from the foul aspects of yesteryears, I pledge myself to persevere in the cultivation of this new, flourishing bond that embodies harmony, compassion, and tenderness.

2015 DTLA SKIDROW
Teri Rogers

Growth and Bridging the Gaps

Through the journey of my existence and the intricate workings of my non-profit organization, I have grasped the subtle significance of growth, self-interrogation, and knitting together the seams between the person I once was and the person I have become. My past travails have imparted upon me invaluable wisdom and have kindled within me an unyielding spirit that propels me forward.

Not exclusively confined to the realm of passionate entanglements, I have traveled in treacherous terrain plagued with the urge of my mind. The presence of past transgressions and the onslaught of contemporary obstacles conspired to drown me in a tidal wave of despair and impotence. It was with grim discernment that I perceived the urgency of safeguarding my emotional sanctity and enlisting the aid to confront the complicated chambers of my mental health.

Through this mission, I found relief in the virtues of accountability and acceptance, both indispensable constituents of the healing chemistry. I took upon myself the shield of responsibility, overcoming before the altar of truth, firmly acknowledging my errors and illnesses. Furthermore, I embraced my authentic self, an act of self-indulgence displaying self-compassion and self-care.

My exploration further endowed upon me the elevation of trust within the knitting of human connections. Trust, that foundational structure upon which all healthy relationships stand, involves honesty, consistency, and dependability. The scar tissue of past traumas and experiences of betrayal once assaulted my ability to trust others. Yet, in my progress, I have acquired the art of cultivating trust through an emotional offering of vulnerability and honesty, coupled with the creation of healthy boundaries to shield my being.

Whilst striving to conquer these personal tribulations, my endeavors grouped with the mission of my non-profit organization—a courageous cause dedicated to breaking the destructive stigmas surrounding mental health, substance abuse, and homelessness. Immersed in this noble pursuit, I found purpose and fulfillment, forging a vessel to channel my energies and attentions towards a compassionate outlook.

One of the most significant voids that separates who I once was and who I have now become resides within my comprehension and acceptance of mental health anxiety. During my formative years, mental illness was an unspoken entity within the confines of my family and community. Therefore, I wrestled with an inability to fathom my torments of despair and unease. Yet, through my warm encounters in romantic involvements and my ceaseless efforts for my non-profit organization, I have realized the utmost significance of addressing mental health with utmost urgency, transcending the perpetual stigma that shrouds it. This enlightenment has empowered me to seek assistance, when necessary, while also creating together a supportive tapestry of resources for fellow individuals navigating comparable hardships.

Paralleling this personal transformation, I have bridged another gap, situated within my perception of the indispensability of effective communication and understanding in the realm of relationships. During my youthful days, I frequently found myself at odds with articulating my needs and emotions, inadvertently inviting misunderstanding and violent turmoil. Yet, my philanthropic quest coupled with the invaluable lessons procured from disputes in previous romantic involvements has infused me with the knowledge of how to eloquently express my thoughts and sentiments in a manner that befits a wholesome and fruitful dialogue. This enlightenment has shown the scope for forming steadfast connections with the individuals populating my existence, effortlessly lacking the misunderstandings and conflicts that once punctuated the shade of my existence, leading me to self-sabotage.

Moreover, alongside the pursuit of personal growth, my professional approach has undergone a momentous changeover. Founding a non-profit institution and successfully attaining a 501(c)3 status has underscored itself as a triumphant milestone, an achievement that seemed wholly uncertain at one time. Absorbed within this sphere of noble labor, I have sharpened my leadership capabilities, refined my fundraising finesse, and pioneered extensive outreach initiatives toward the community at large. These newfound competencies have fit favorably with my aspirations to eradicate stigmatization surrounding mental health, substance use disorder, and homelessness, serving as pipelines for fostering a positive resonance within my community and propelling me closer to the realization of my objectives.

The film's ending finds me and the other protagonist, an inseparable duo, hovering in the chambers of uncertainty. Meanwhile, I am resolute in my pursuit of personal growth and refinement, the other protagonist appears content with an existence tethered to the gloom of Skid Row. As the closing credits slither across the screen, spectators are left wrestling with their ideas, pondering whether the desire between these companions will persist, triumphing over the overwhelming obstacles they confront.

In the noble swag of "Game Girls," a remarkable and moving creation resonates, emphasizing the awful trials endured by those cut off upon the misery-filled streets of Skid Row. The chronicle of the documentary masterpiece exposes the unawareness surrounding harmful addictions, unstable mental well-being, and the haunting repercussions of previous traumas upon the sacred grounds of fellowship. Simultaneously, it delivers upon us a weighty insight into the treasured essence of love and solidarity while on the grueling mission towards revival and redemption.

Resident at court Mandated Treatment Facility 2022
Teri Rogers

Conclusion

As I bring my journey to a close, I am compelled to reflect upon the manifold challenges and trials that have highlighted my path. Yet, with steadfast determination, introspection, and an enthusiastic aspiration to aid fellow beings, I have managed to travel an exhausting road. Painfully, my encounters have served as catalysts to fuel the kick-off of a nonprofit organization aimed at shattering the debilitating misconceptions surrounding these predicaments and proffering indispensable support to those yearning for relief.

From the crucible of my strife and afflictions, I have imbibed invaluable lessons on responsibility, acceptance, effective communication, and self-nurturance. subsequently, my dedication lies in the interpretation of my intense personal chronicle and zealous advocacy for the illumination of society regarding mental well-being, liberation from substance abuse, bolstering the destitute, engendering financial enlightenment, and extending legal assistance.

It is my heartfelt aspiration that through the conveyance of my narrative and encounters, fortitude shall be instilled within others, impelling them to seek comfort and support. Also, my dream resides in the transformation of societal attitudes, eradicating the onerous prejudices and bestowing the necessary provisions upon those ensnared in unfortunate circumstances. In spirited unity, we can conceive a realm that proffers impartiality and justice to every individual, irrespective of the adversities that beset their existence.

RESOURCES

https://dpss.lacounty.gov/en.html

https://www.hud.gov/topics/housing_choice_voucher_program_section_8

https://www.lacourt.org/onlineservices/on0001.aspx

http://dmh.lacounty.gov/

http://www.youthcrisisline.org/

http://www.teenlineonline.org/

https://www.google.com/search?q=homeboy+industries&ie=UTF-8&oe=UTF-8&hl=en-us&client=safari

https://anewwayoflife.org/

https://www.tarzanatc.org/

https://www.dor.ca.gov/

https://stjosephctr.org/

https://www.shieldsforfamilies.org/

https://www.2ndcall.org/

https://www.socialmodelrecovery.org/

https://shareselfhelp.org/

https://www.exodusrecovery.com/

https://locator.lacounty.gov/dmh/Location/3181371/womens-community-reintegration-and-education-center

https://www.samhsa.gov/find-help/national-helpline

https://lacoaa.org/

https://stigmas.info/

Game Girls Reviews

Documentary 'Game Girls' sheds light on life and love on the streets of Skid ... https://abc7.com/amp/skid-row-documentary-game-girls-love-story/3756846/

Let's Really Talk About Homelessness - Los Angeles Sentinel https://lasentinel.net/lets-really-talk-about-homelessness.html

'Game Girls' review - The Hollywood Reporter https://www.hollywoodreporter.com/movies/movie-reviews/game-girls-review-1084222/amp/

Alina Skrzeszewska, Director of 'Game Girls' Doc Talks Skid Row - Variety https://variety.com/2018/film/news/berlin-profile-alina-skrzeszewska-director-of-game-girls-doc-talks-skid-row-1202694417/amp/

Reviews: Raw docs 'Game Girls' and 'Origin Story,' plus the suicide drama ... https://www.latimes.com/entertainment/movies/la-et-mn-capsule2-review-string-20190510-story.html

Game Girls: A Poetic Take on Skid Row Documentary | Art-bound - PBS SoCal https://www.pbssocal.org/shows/artbound/game-girls-a-poetic-take-on-skid-row-documentary

https://filmthreat.com/reviews/game-girls/

https://www.peoplesworld.org/article/game-girls-an-unfiltered-documentary-on-being-black-lesbian-and-homeless/

https://afterellen.com/game-girls-review-black-lesbian/

https://cineuropa.org/en/newsdetail/348255/

https://moveablefest.com/alina-skrzeszewska-game-girls/

https://www.theupcoming.co.uk/2018/02/20/berlin-film-festival-2018-game-girls-review/

Game Girls | International Documentary Association https://www.documentary.org/project/game-girls

FESTIVALS & AWARDS

2019

Some Prefer Cake (**Italia**)

Festival Echos d'ici, échos d'ailleurs (**France**)

2018

Watch Docs – International Human Rights Film Festival (**Poland**)

This Human World – International Human Rights Film Festival (**Austria**)

Traces de vies – Regard documentaire hors frontières (**France**)

Image de Ville (**France**)

Festival Chéries-Chéris (**France**)

Gijon International Film Festival – *Award CIMA best film by female director* (**Spain**)

Festival Dei Popoli – International competition (**Italia**)

Corsica.doc – New talents competition (**France**)

ZeFestival (**France**)

FIFIB International Festival of Indépendant Film of Bordeaux – *Grand Prix du Jury* (**France**)

Filmfestival Kitzbühel (**Austria**)

États Généraux du Documentaire de Lussas – Expérience du Regard (**France**)

Outfest Los Angeles (**United States**)

Sheffield Doc Fest (**England**)

Festival international du film de femmes de Séoul (**South Korea**)

Festival international du film de Thessalonique (**Greece**)

Berlinale – Panorama – Wolrd Premiere (**Germany**)

**I would like to take this moment to personally
Thank You
for your time, interest and contribution towards
bringing awareness and breaking stigmas in our
communities.**

If you would like to DONATE, you can do so by scanning QR CODE
below.

A portion of your generous donations will also go toward assisting

Women, Men, Senior Citizens and The Youth in Recovery.

"FREE WORLD"

Teri was born on November 13, 1980, and currently resides in Los Angeles, California. As the oldest of four children and the only girl, she developed a passion for caretaking and cooking while helping her parents around the house. She credits her family for instilling certain values that have guided her throughout her life journey. In 2015, Teri came across a flyer advertising a free workshop for women living in the "SKIDROW" area of downtown Los Angeles. Little did she know, that moment would change her life. "My mission, says Teri, is to break the stigmas associated with Mental Health, Substance Abuse, Homelessness, and STIs (Sexually Transmitted Infections). Iaim to provide housing, therapeutic activities, support groups, and regular treatment plans coordinated by individuals and licensed professionals. I also use my documentary "Game Girls" as a platform to inspire, encourage, motivate, advocate, uplift, educate, and be the voice for others. I strive to be the light at the end of the tunnel."

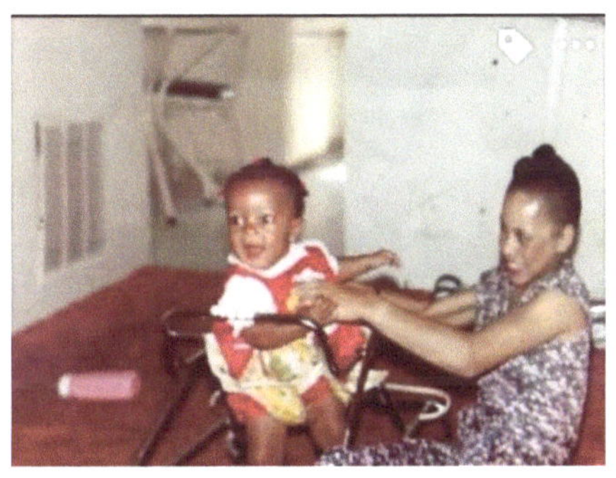

1981
Teri & Mommy

1990 Glamour Shot
Teri Rogers

1999 H.S. Graduation
Teri Rogers

1996
Teri Rogers